'My Pet' and 'Full Bed'
An original concept by Rebecca Colby
© Rebecca Colby 2023

Illustrated by Denis Alonso (Beehive Illustration)

Published by MAVERICK ARTS PUBLISHING LTD

Studio 11, City Business Centre, 6 Brighton Road,

Horsham, West Sussex, RH13 5BB

© Maverick Arts Publishing Limited February 2023

+44 (0)1403 256941

A CIP catalogue record for this book is available at the British Library.

ISBN 978-1-84886-925-7

www.maverickbooks.co.uk

Pink

This book is rated as: Pink Band (Guided Reading)
It follows the requirements for Phase 2 phonics.
Most words are decodable, and any non-decodable words are familiar, supported by the context and/or represented in the artwork.

My Pet

and

Full Bed

By Rebecca
Colby

Illustrated by
Denis Alonso

The Letter E

Trace the lower and upper case letter with a finger. Sound out the letter.

Across,
around

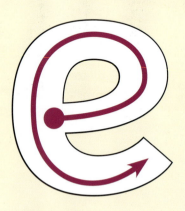

Down,
lift, cross,
lift, cross,
lift, cross

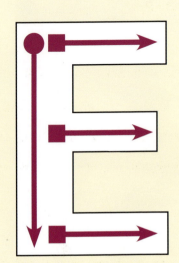

Some words to familiarise:

bat   rat   rabbit

High-frequency words:

is   it   a

this   my

Tips for Reading 'My Pet'

- Practise the words listed above before reading the story.

- If the reader struggles with any of the other words, ask them to look for sounds they know in the word. Encourage them to sound out the words and help them read the words if necessary.

- After reading the story, ask the reader what the last pet was.

Fun Activity

Discuss! If you could have any pet, what would it be?

My Pet

This is my pet.
It is a cat.

The Letter F

Trace the lower and upper case letter with a finger. Sound out the letter.

Around,
down,
lift,
cross

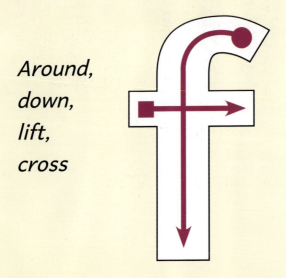

Down,
lift,
cross,
lift,
cross

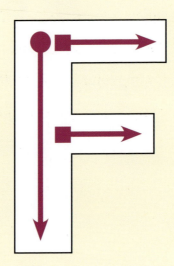

Some words to familiarise:

bed   Tuff   full

High-frequency words:

is   in   the

Tips for Reading 'Full Bed'

- Practise the words listed above before reading the story.

- If the reader struggles with any of the other words, ask them to look for sounds they know in the word. Encourage them to sound out the words and help them read the words if necessary.

- After reading the story, ask the reader how many dragons were in Dot's bed.

Fun Activity

Draw a dragon!

Full Bed

Huff is not in bed.

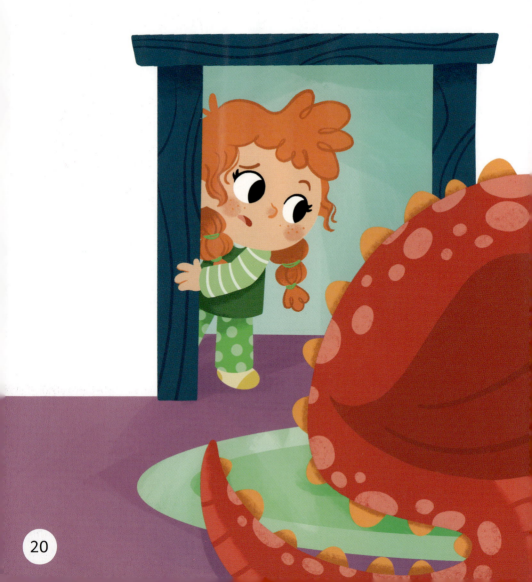

Puff is not in bed.

Ruff is not in bed.

Tuff is not in bed.

Dot is in bed.

Huff, Puff, Ruff and Tuff
are in bed.

The bed is full.

Book Bands for Guided Reading

The Institute of Education book banding system is a scale of colours that reflects the various levels of reading difficulty. The bands are assigned by taking into account the content, the language style, the layout and phonics. Word, phrase and sentence level work is also taken into consideration.

Maverick Early Readers are a bright, attractive range of books covering the pink to white bands. All of these books have been book banded for guided reading to the industry standard and edited by a leading educational consultant.

Pink

Red

Yellow

Blue

Green

Orange

Turquoise

Purple

Gold

White

To view the whole Maverick Readers scheme, visit our website at www.maverickearlyreaders.com

Or scan the QR code above to view our scheme instantly!